a gift to

_____

from

_____

i am THE DOG

Published by KPT Publishing
Minneapolis, Minnesota 55406
www.KPTPublishing.com

ISBN 978-1-944833-01-5

Design by David Abeler
Production by Koechel Peterson and Associates, Minneapolis, Minnesota

First printing March 2017

10 9 8 7 6 5 4

Printed in the United States of America

UNCONDITIONAL LOVE

I track in dirt.

I vigilantly check your garden for moles.

I leave you hidden treats in the yard.

I bark to protect you from shadows and squirrels.

I sleep on your bed to make sure you keep warm.

I emphasize my affection by drooling.

I love my food AND your food!

I checked and your new shoes are decent chew toys, even if they don't squeak like my other ones.

What's there *not* to love?

Maybe you didn't realize…

*but I know
where you
keep your socks.*

C'mon, admit it...
You love me.

I've got all day.

Laugh at my nose
all you want...

smell your pillow.

Remember,
I've already
forgiven
and forgotten
I've done it.

Can we go now?

Why is my tail
so curly?

To keep
"the happy" *in*
as long as possible.

You've had a tough day.
I've got the leash.
Let's go for a walk
and you can
tell me all about it.

No, really,
it was CRAZY!
Your shoe…
Well I barely escaped!
But you're safe now.

I must say,
I do envy those dogs
with the really long ears
right now.

Put the
window down *more*…
and go *faster!*

Stop asking me
"Who's the pretty boy?"

At least the curlers
aren't pink.

Wanna know
a secret?
I love your cat,
we're snuggle
buds.

They say an owner starts looking like his pet.

"And I'm gorgeous!"

This rain is washing away all of *my* territory!

I know the sound
of your car...

9 blocks away.

"Bad dog."
What do you mean
"bad dog?"

You didn't even notice
that I found
your tv remote.

I'll love you more
in a few minutes.
I just need to
rest first.

"Wet dog" *is* still better than skunk.

You really believe
I can actually
reach the top of that
waste basket?

Loyalty and me
go together like
"man"
and
"best friend"

Here's that perfectly good stick you keep throwing away.

What do you mean
"where's the ball?"

I just saw you
throw it
over there?

I saw suitcases.

Did I do something wrong?

Imagine...
the terrible two's...
times five.

Just do what
my dad taught me.

Pee on it
then find
another one.

You did say
you were done
with this,
right?

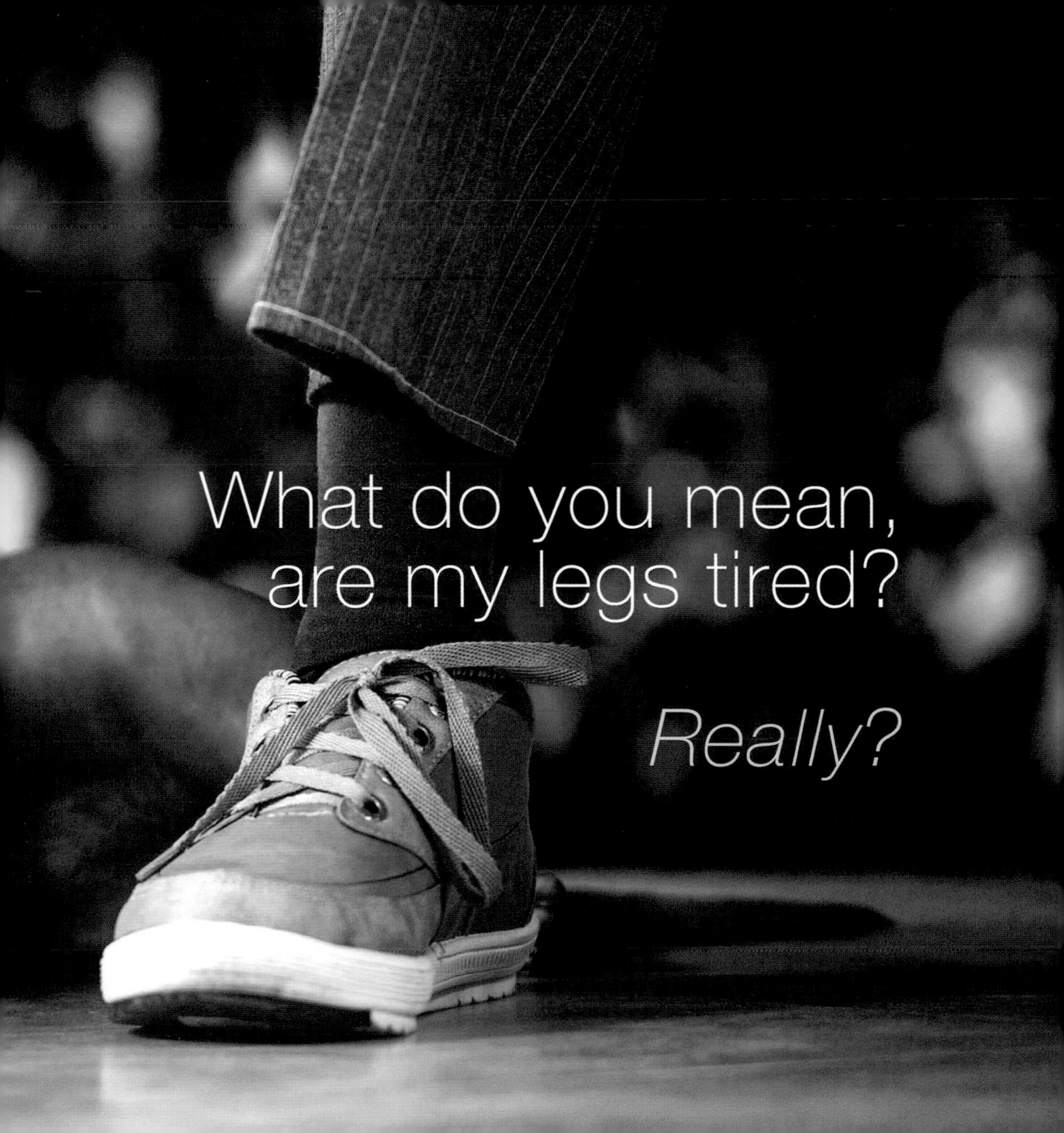
What do you mean,
are my legs tired?
Really?

I'm *nicer* than
the average person
you meet.

I'm not just
a pretty face.
I have
super powers!

I can tell
who loves me!

Until next time…

ABOUT THE AUTHOR

LIZ ABELER BLAYLOCK lives in Minnesota with her husband and cat.
She called on the assistance of her brother and his family—dog lovers—
to bring about this story: life with a dog.

> *"I marvel at the intricate, beautiful and fearful working
> of creation, and revel in the grace and mercy of the Creator."*

Hope you enjoyed the memories!